Ulrich Renz / Barbara B

Čuči saldi, ma

Sleep Tight, Little Wolf

Bilžu grāmata divās valodās

Tulkojums:

Līga Hirta (latviešu)

Pete Savill (angļu)

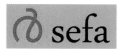
sefa

Download audiobook at:

www.sefa-bilingual.com/mp3

Password for free access:

latviešu: **audiogrāmata vēl nav pieejama**

angļu: **LWEN1423**

"Ar labu nakti, Tim! Rīt meklēsim tālāk.

Tagad čuči saldi!"

"Good night, Tim! We'll continue searching tomorrow.

Now sleep tight!"

Ārā ir jau satumsis.

It is already dark outside.

Ko gan Tims tur dara?

What is Tim doing?

Viņš iet ārā uz spēļu laukumu.

Ko gan viņš tur meklē?

He is leaving for the playground.

What is he looking for there?

Mazo vilciņu!

Bez tā viņš nevar aizmigt.

The little wolf!

He can't sleep without it.

Kas gan tur nāk?

Who's this coming?

Marī!

Viņa meklē savu bumbu.

Marie!

She's looking for her ball.

Un ko meklē Tobī?

And what is Tobi looking for?

Savu ekskavatoru.

His digger.

Un ko meklē Nala?

And what is Nala looking for?

Savu lelli.

Her doll.

Vai gan bērniem nebūtu jābūt gultā?

Kaķis ir ļoti izbrīnīts.

Don't the children have to go to bed?

The cat is rather surprised.

Un kas gan tagad tur nāk?

Who's coming now?

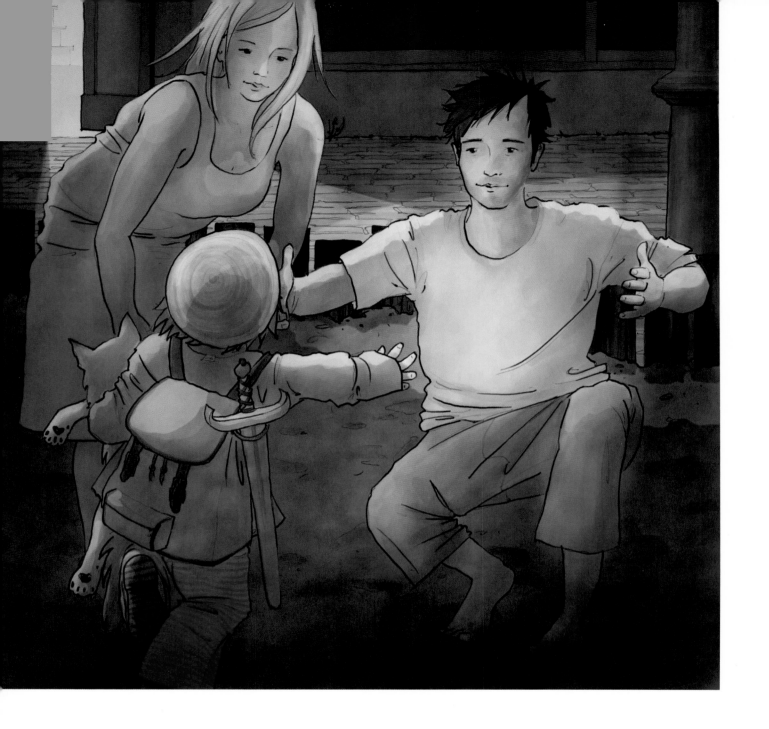

Tima mamma un tētis!
Bez sava Tima viņi nevar aizmigt.

Tim's mum and dad!
They can't sleep without their Tim.

Un re – nāk vēl citi! Marī tētis.

Tobī opis. Un Nalas mamma.

More of them are coming! Marie's dad.

Tobi's grandpa. And Nala's mum.

Bet tagad gan – žigli gultiņā!

Now hurry to bed everyone!

"Ar labu nakti, Tim!
Rīt mums vairs nevajadzēs meklēt."

"Good night, Tim!
Tomorrow we won't have to search any longer."

Čuči saldi, mazo vilciņ!

Sleep tight, little wolf!

More about me ...

Que duermas bien, pequeño lobo
Schlaf gut, kleiner Wolf
Ulrich Renz / Barbara Brinkmann
español · bilingüe · alemán

Schlaf gut, kleiner Wolf
راحت بخواب، گرگ کوچک
Ulrich Renz / Barbara Brinkmann
Deutsch · bilingual · Persisch (Farsi)

Dors bien, petit loup
Sleep Tight, Little Wolf
Ulrich Renz / Barbara Brinkmann
français · bilingue · anglais

نم جيدا أيها الذئب الصغير
Sov gott, lilla vargen
Ulrich Renz / Barbara Brinkmann
العربية · ثنائي اللغة · السويدية

Sofðu rótt, litli úlfur
Όνειρα γλυκά, μικρέ λύκε
Ulrich Renz / Barbara Brinkmann
íslenska · tvímála · gríska

Dorme bem, lobinho
Suaviter dormi, lupe parve
Ulrich Renz / Barbara Brinkmann
português · bilingue · latino

Schlaf gut, kleiner Wolf
おおかみくんも
ぐっすり おやすみなさい
Ulrich Renz / Barbara Brinkmann
Deutsch · bilingual · Japanisch

잘 자, 꼬마 늑대야
Slaap lekker, kleine wolf
Ulrich Renz / Barbara Brinkmann
한국어 · 양국어 · 네덜란드어

Приятных снов, маленький волчёнок
Sleep Tight, Little Wolf
Ulrich Renz / Barbara Brinkmann
русский · двуязычный · английский

راحت بخواب، گرگ کوچک
Schlaf gut, kleiner Wolf
Ulrich Renz / Barbara Brinkmann
فارسی · دوزبانی · آلمانی

Que duermas bien, pequeño lobo
نم جيداً أيها الذئب الصغير
Ulrich Renz / Barbara Brinkmann
español · bilingüe · árabe

സുഖമായി ഉറങ്ങൂ
ചെന്നായി കുഞ്ഞേ
Dormi bene, piccolo lupo
Ulrich Renz / Barbara Brinkmann
മലയാളം · ദ്വിഭാഷ · ഇറ്റാലിയൻ

Dormi bene, piccolo lupo
जम के सोना , छोटे भेड़िये
Ulrich Renz / Barbara Brinkmann
italiano · bilingue · hindi

ፁቡቀ ድቃስ፡ ንእሽቶይ ተኹላ
Selamat tidur, si serigala
Ulrich Renz / Barbara Brinkmann
ትግራ · ዜ ዛወ ቛኔ · Malaysian

Śpij dobrze, mały wilku
ძილო ნებისა, პატარა მგელო
Ulrich Renz / Barbara Brinkmann
polski · Dwujęzyczna · gruziński

Солодких снів, маленький вовчику
잘 자, 꼬마 늑대야
Ulrich Renz / Barbara Brinkmann
українська · двомовний · корейська

Children's Books for the Global Village

Ever more children are born away from their parents' home countries, and are balancing between the languages of their mother, their father, their grandparents, and their peers. Our bilingual books are meant to help bridge the language divides that cross more and more families, neighborhoods and kindergartens in the globalized world.

Little Wolf also proposes:

The Wild Swans

Bilingual picture book
adapted from
a fairy tale by
Hans Christian Andersen

► Reading age 4 and up

www.childrens-books-bilingual.com

Home	Authors	Little Wolf	About

Bilingual Children's Books - in any language you want

Welcome to Little Wolf's Language Wizard!

Just choose the two languages in which you want to read to your children:

Language 1:

French ⌄

Language 2:

Icelandic ⌄

Go!

Learn more about our bilingual books at www.childrens-books-bilingual.com. At the heart of this website you will find what we call our "Language Wizard". It contains more than 60 languages and any of their bilingual combinations: Just select, in a simple drop-down-menu, the two languages in which you'd like to read "Little Wolf" or "The Wild Swans" to your child – and the book is instantly made available, ready for order as an ebook download or as a printed edition.

As time goes by ...

... the little ones grow older, and start to read on their own. Here is Little Wolf's recommendation to them:

BO & FRIENDS

Smart detective stories for smart children

Reading age: 10 + - www.bo-and-friends.com

Wie die Zeit vergeht ...

Irgendwann sind aus den süßen Kleinen süße Große geworden
– die jetzt sogar selber lesen können. Der kleine Wolf empfiehlt:

MOTTE & CO

Kinderkrimis zum Mitdenken

Lesealter ab 10 – www.motte-und-co.de

About the authors

Ulrich Renz was born in Stuttgart, Germany, in 1960. After studying French literature in Paris he graduated from medical school in Lübeck and worked as head of a scientific publishing company. He is now a writer of non-fiction books as well as children's fiction books. – www.ulrichrenz.de

Barbara Brinkmann was born in Munich, Germany, in 1969. She grew up in the foothills of the Alps and studied architecture and medicine for a while in Munich. She now works as a freelance graphic artist, illustrator and writer. – www.bcbrinkmann.com

© 2018 by Sefa Verlag Kirsten Bödeker, Lübeck, Germany
www.sefa-verlag.de

sefa

IT: Paul Bödeker, München, Germany
Font: Noto Sans

ISBN: 9783739944456

Version: 20180225

Printed by Amazon Italia Logistica S.r.l.
Torrazza Piemonte (TO), Italy

11688712R00016